Dedications

1. This book is dedicated to my lovely wife Julie who supports my many crazy ideas…most of the time.

2. Also, the book is dedicated to all those who have suffered, are suffering, and may suffer from mental unwellness. You are not alone!

3. Google Images 2024 for the pictures in the text.

Table of Contents

Chapter 1: Understanding Holistic Mental Health   4

What is Holistic Mental Health?   4

The Connection Between Mind, Body, Social and Spirit   5

Traditional vs. Holistic Approaches to Mental Wellness   7

Chapter 2: Assessing Your Mental Health Needs   9

Identifying Your Triggers and Stressors   9

Evaluating Your Current Mental Health Status   10

Creating a Personalized Mental Health Plan   12

Chapter 3: Holistic Therapies for Mental Wellness   14

Meditation and Mindfulness Practices   14

Yoga and Movement Therapy   15

Nutrition and Mental Health   17

Chapter 4: Healing from Within   19

Self-Care Practices for Mental Wellness   19

Building a Support System   20

Practicing Gratitude and Mindfulness   22

Chapter 5: Finding Balance in Daily Life   24

Time Management and Prioritizing Self-Care   24

Setting Boundaries and Saying No   25

Incorporating Holistic Practices into Your Routine   26

Chapter 6: Overcoming Mental Health Stigma   28

Educating Yourself and Others   28

Advocating for Mental Health Awareness   29

Embracing Your Journey to Wellness   31

Chapter 7: Maintaining Holistic Mental Health   33

Monitoring Your Progress and Adjusting Your Plan   33

Continuing Education and Growth   34

Celebrating Your Successes and Practicing Self-Compassion   36

Chapter 8: Resources for Holistic Mental Health   39

Finding Holistic Mental Health Practitioners   39

Recommended Reading and Websites   40

Support Groups and Community Resources   42

Conclusion: Embracing Your Journey to Holistic Mental Health   44

The Four Dimensions of Hauora (Holistic Wellbeing)   46

Explanation and Diagram   46-47

Chapter 1: Understanding Holistic Mental Health

What is Holistic Mental Health?

In this subchapter, we will explore the concept of holistic mental health and how it differs from traditional approaches to mental wellness. Holistic mental health is a comprehensive approach to mental wellness that takes into account the interconnectedness of the mind, body, social, and spirit. It recognizes that mental health is not just about treating symptoms, but about addressing the underlying causes of mental illness.

Holistic mental health focuses on treating the whole person, rather than just the symptoms of mental illness. This means taking into account a person's physical health, emotional well-being, social relationships, and spiritual beliefs. By addressing all aspects of a person's life, holistic mental health can help individuals achieve greater balance and well-being.

One of the key principles of holistic mental health is the belief that mental health is influenced by a variety of factors, including diet, exercise, sleep, stress levels, and relationships.

By addressing these factors, individuals can improve their mental health and overall well-being. Holistic approaches to mental wellness may include therapies such as mindfulness meditation, yoga, acupuncture, nutrition counselling, and energy healing.

Holistic mental health also emphasizes the importance of self-care and self-awareness. By taking the time to care for us and listen to our own needs, we can better manage our mental health and prevent future episodes of mental illness. Holistic approaches to mental wellness encourage individuals to take an active role in their own healing process and empower them to make positive changes in their lives.

Overall, holistic mental health offers a more comprehensive and personalized approach to mental wellness that can benefit individuals suffering from mental illness. By addressing the mind, body, social, and spirit, holistic approaches to mental health can help individuals achieve greater balance, resilience, and well-being. It is important for those struggling with mental illness to consider holistic approaches to mental wellness as part of their overall treatment plan.

The Connection Between Mind, Body, Social and Spirit

The connection between mind, body, and spirit is a fundamental aspect of holistic mental health. In order to achieve true balance and well-being, it is essential to address all four components of our being. When one aspect is out of alignment, it can have a negative impact on the others, leading to mental health issues such as anxiety, depression, and stress. By understanding and nurturing the connection between mind, body, and spirit, individuals can experience greater harmony and peace in their lives. In Māori culture in New Zealand this connection is referred to as Hauora - it is the Māori word for health and wellbeing. The four walls of a Whare, a sacred Māori meeting house are used to represent the four dimensions of Hauora (refer to back page 24 for explanation and diagram).

The mind plays a crucial role in our mental health, as it is where our thoughts, beliefs, and emotions reside. Negative thought patterns and limiting beliefs can create mental distress and lead to symptoms of anxiety and depression. By practicing mindfulness and cognitive behavioural techniques, individuals can learn to challenge and reframe these negative thoughts, promoting a healthier mental state. It is important to cultivate a positive mindset and practice self-compassion in order to support mental well-being.

The body is another essential component of holistic mental health, as physical health, social health, and mental health are closely intertwined. Regular exercise, proper nutrition, and adequate sleep are all important factors in maintaining a healthy body and mind. Physical activity has been shown to reduce symptoms of depression and anxiety, while a balanced diet can provide the nutrients needed for optimal brain function. By taking care of our bodies, we can support our mental health and overall well-being.

Social relationships play a vitally important role in holistic mental health. Individuals need human contact and relationships with family (whanau), friends, and significant others. Without these, they may suffer from loneliness, anxiety, or depression, leading to social isolation. Having positive relationships can build confidence and the desire to seek social encounters, thus, building social wellbeing.

Spirituality is often overlooked in traditional mental health approaches, but it plays a significant role in holistic wellness. Connecting with a higher power, practicing meditation, or engaging in spiritual practices can provide individuals with a sense of purpose, meaning, and inner peace. Spirituality can also help individuals cope with stress, trauma, and life challenges, providing a source of strength and resilience. By nurturing the spiritual aspect of our being, we can find greater balance and harmony in our lives.

In conclusion, the connection between mind, body, social, and spirit is vital to achieving holistic mental health. By addressing all these components of our being, individuals can experience greater well-being, inner peace, and resilience in the face of life's challenges. Through mindfulness, self-care, and spiritual practices, people suffering from mental illness can cultivate a sense of balance and harmony in their lives. By embracing a holistic approach to mental wellness, individuals can support their mental health and overall well-being.

Traditional vs. Holistic Approaches to Mental Wellness

In the world of mental health treatment, there are two main approaches that individuals can choose from when seeking help for their mental wellness: traditional and holistic. Traditional approaches typically involve therapy, medication, and other interventions that are rooted in Western medicine and psychology. On the other hand, holistic approaches focus on treating the whole person - mind, body, social, and spirit - through alternative therapies such as acupuncture, yoga, meditation, and nutrition.

For people suffering from mental illness, it can be overwhelming to navigate the vast array of treatment options available. Traditional approaches, such as therapy and medication, are often the first line of defence for many individuals seeking relief from symptoms of anxiety, depression, and other mental health conditions. While these methods can be effective for some people, others may find that they do not provide the comprehensive care they need to truly heal.

Holistic approaches to mental wellness, on the other hand, offer a more integrated and personalized approach to treatment. By addressing the underlying causes of mental illness and incorporating alternative therapies that promote overall well-being, holistic treatments can help individuals achieve a more balanced and sustainable state of mental health. For example, practices like yoga and meditation can help individuals manage stress and anxiety, while acupuncture and nutrition can support the body's natural healing processes.

One of the key differences between traditional and holistic approaches to mental wellness is the emphasis on prevention and self-care. While traditional treatments often focus on symptom management, holistic approaches aim to empower individuals to take control of their own mental health and well-being. This can involve making lifestyle changes, such as incorporating regular exercise, healthy eating, and mindfulness practices into daily routines.

Ultimately, the choice between traditional and holistic approaches to mental wellness is a personal one that should be based on individual needs and preferences. For some people, a combination of both traditional and holistic treatments may be the most effective approach to achieving mental wellness. By exploring the different options available and working with a qualified healthcare provider, individuals can find the right path to healing and balance for their mental health.

Chapter 2: Assessing Your Mental Health Needs

Identifying Your Triggers and Stressors

In order to effectively manage your mental health, it is crucial to identify the triggers and stressors that contribute to your symptoms. Triggers are specific events or situations that cause a negative reaction or exacerbate existing mental health issues. Stressors, on the other hand, are ongoing sources of stress that can wear down your mental resilience over time. By pinpointing these triggers and stressors, you can take proactive steps to reduce their impact on your mental well-being.

One way to identify your triggers and stressors is to keep a journal and track your moods and reactions to various situations. Pay attention to patterns and common themes that emerge – are there certain people, places, or activities that consistently trigger negative emotions? Are there specific stressors in your life that seem to be taking a toll on your mental health? By documenting these patterns, you can gain valuable insights into the factors that contribute to your mental health struggles.

Another helpful strategy for identifying triggers and stressors is to seek feedback from trusted friends, family members, or mental health professionals. Sometimes, those closest to us can offer valuable perspectives on our behaviour and reactions that we may not be able to see ourselves. By opening up to others about your struggles, you can gain new insights and perspectives that can help you identify and address your triggers and stressors more effectively.

Once you have identified your triggers and stressors, it is important to develop coping strategies to help you manage them more effectively. This may involve setting boundaries with toxic people or situations, practicing stress-reducing techniques such as mindfulness or meditation, or seeking professional help from a therapist or counsellor. By taking proactive steps to address your triggers and stressors, you can reduce their impact on your mental health and improve your overall well-being.

In conclusion, identifying your triggers and stressors is a crucial step in managing your mental health and finding balance in your life. By keeping a journal, seeking feedback from others, and developing coping strategies, you can gain a deeper understanding of the factors that contribute to your mental health struggles and take proactive steps to address them. Remember, you are not alone in this journey – there are resources and support available to help you navigate the challenges of mental illness and achieve holistic mental wellness.

Evaluating Your Current Mental Health Status

Assessing your current mental health status is an essential step in the journey towards holistic wellness. As someone suffering from mental illness, it is crucial to take the time to reflect on your emotional, psychological, and spiritual well-being. By evaluating where you currently stand, you can gain valuable insights into areas that may need improvement and develop a personalized plan for achieving balance and harmony in your life.

One way to evaluate your mental health status is to take stock of your emotions on a regular basis. Pay attention to how you are feeling throughout the day and identify any patterns or triggers that may be impacting your mood. By keeping a journal or using a mood tracking app, you can gain a better understanding of your emotional fluctuations and take proactive steps to address any negative feelings that arise.

Another important aspect of evaluating your mental health status is assessing your thoughts and beliefs. Our thoughts have a powerful impact on our emotions and behaviours, so it is essential to examine any negative or self-defeating beliefs that may be contributing to your mental illness. By challenging these beliefs and replacing them with more positive and empowering thoughts, you can begin to shift your mindset towards one of self-compassion and self-acceptance.

In addition to emotions and thoughts, it is also important to evaluate your physical health when assessing your mental wellness. Research has shown that there is a strong connection between the body and mind, so taking care of your physical health through proper nutrition, exercise, and sleep can have a positive impact on your mental well-being. By incorporating holistic practices such as yoga, meditation, and mindfulness into your daily routine, you can promote overall wellness and support your mental health.

Lastly, evaluating your current mental health status involves assessing your support system and seeking help when needed. Surrounding yourself with a strong network of friends, family, and mental health professionals can provide you with the guidance and support you need to navigate the challenges of mental illness. By reaching out for help and building a support system that understands and validates your experience, you can create a safe and nurturing environment for healing and growth. Remember, you are not alone in your journey towards holistic mental wellness, and there are resources available to support you every step of the way.

Creating a Personalized Mental Health Plan

Creating a personalized mental health plan is essential for those suffering from mental illness, as it allows individuals to tailor their treatment and support to meet their unique needs. One size does not fit all when it comes to mental health, and finding what works best for you is crucial in finding balance and healing. In this subchapter, we will explore how to develop a personalized mental health plan that incorporates holistic approaches to mental wellness.

The first step in creating a personalized mental health plan is to assess your current mental health status. This may involve meeting with a mental health professional, such as a therapist or psychiatrist, to discuss your symptoms, triggers, and overall mental well-being. By gaining a better understanding of where you are currently at, you can begin to identify areas that need improvement and set goals for your mental health journey.

Once you have assessed your mental health status, the next step is to identify your strengths and resources. This may include support systems such as friends, family, or community organizations, as well as coping mechanisms and skills that have helped you in the past. By recognizing and utilizing your strengths and resources, you can build a strong foundation for your personalized mental health plan.

Incorporating holistic approaches to mental wellness into your personalized mental health plan is also crucial. Holistic approaches take into account the interconnectedness of mind, body, and spirit, and focus on treating the whole person rather than just the symptoms of mental illness. This may include practices such as meditation, yoga, nutrition, exercise, and mindfulness, all of which can have a positive impact on mental health.

Finally, it is important to regularly review and adjust your personalized mental health plan as needed. Mental health is not static, and what works for you now may not work in the future. By staying flexible and open to trying new approaches, you can continue to evolve and grow on your mental health journey. Remember, you are in control of your mental health, and by creating a personalized mental health plan that aligns with your needs and values, you can find balance and healing in your life.

Chapter 3: Holistic Therapies for Mental Wellness

Meditation and Mindfulness Practices

In this subchapter, we will explore the powerful benefits of meditation and mindfulness practices for individuals suffering from mental illness. These holistic approaches to mental wellness can provide relief from symptoms such as anxiety, depression, and stress, while promoting overall emotional and mental well-being.

Meditation is a practice that involves focusing the mind on a particular object, thought, or activity in order to achieve a state of mental clarity and emotional calmness. For individuals struggling with mental illness, meditation can be a valuable tool for managing symptoms and improving overall mental health. By quieting the mind and cultivating a sense of inner peace, meditation can help individuals develop greater self-awareness and emotional resilience.

Mindfulness, on the other hand, involves paying purposeful attention to the present moment without judgment. This practice encourages individuals to acknowledge and accept their thoughts, feelings, and sensations without becoming overwhelmed by them. Mindfulness can help individuals with mental illness develop a greater sense of self-compassion and acceptance, while reducing rumination and negative self-talk.

Research has shown that meditation and mindfulness practices can have a significant impact on mental health outcomes. Studies have found that these practices can reduce symptoms of anxiety and depression, improve cognitive functioning, and enhance overall well-being. By incorporating meditation and mindfulness into their daily routines, individuals suffering from mental illness can experience greater emotional stability and a deeper sense of inner peace.

In conclusion, meditation and mindfulness practices offer powerful tools for individuals struggling with mental illness. By incorporating these holistic approaches into their daily routines, individuals can experience relief from symptoms, improve emotional well-being, and cultivate greater self-awareness and resilience. Through regular practice, individuals can find balance and peace of mind in the midst of their struggles, ultimately leading to improved mental health and overall well-being.

Yoga and Movement Therapy

Yoga and movement therapy are powerful tools for promoting holistic mental health and well-being. By combining physical movement with mindfulness and breathwork, these practices can help individuals suffering from mental illness find balance and healing. In this subchapter, we will explore the benefits of yoga and movement therapy for mental wellness and provide practical tips for incorporating these practices into your daily routine.

Yoga has been used for centuries to promote physical, mental, and emotional well-being. Through a series of postures, breathwork, and meditation, yoga helps individuals cultivate awareness of their bodies and minds. This heightened awareness can help people suffering from mental illness identify and address negative thought patterns, reduce stress and anxiety, and improve overall mental health. By incorporating yoga into your daily routine, you can create a sense of calm and balance that can help you navigate the challenges of mental illness with greater ease.

Movement therapy is another powerful tool for promoting mental wellness. By engaging in physical movement, individuals can release pent-up emotions, reduce stress, and improve mood. Movement therapy can take many forms, from dance and tai chi to walking and swimming. The key is to find a form of movement that resonates with you and helps you connect with your body and emotions. By incorporating movement therapy into your daily routine, you can release tension, increase energy levels, and promote a sense of well-being that can support your mental health journey.

Practicing yoga and movement therapy can also help individuals suffering from mental illness develop a greater sense of self-compassion and self-care. By taking the time to move your body, breathe deeply, and connect with your inner self, you can cultivate a sense of kindness and acceptance toward yourself. This self-compassion can help you navigate the challenges of mental illness with greater resilience and self-awareness. By prioritizing your mental wellness through yoga and movement therapy, you can create a foundation of self-care that can support your healing journey.

In conclusion, yoga and movement therapy are powerful tools for promoting holistic mental health and well-being. By incorporating these practices into your daily routine, you can cultivate awareness, reduce stress, and promote self-compassion. Whether you choose to practice yoga, dance, or simply take a walk-in nature, finding a form of movement that resonates with you can support your mental health journey. Remember to be gentle with yourself as you explore these practices and to listen to your body's needs. By prioritizing your mental wellness through yoga and movement therapy, you can find balance and healing on your path to holistic mental health.

Nutrition and Mental Health

Nutrition plays a crucial role in our mental health and overall well-being. The food we eat directly impacts our brain function, mood, and energy levels. For individuals suffering from mental illness, making conscious choices about their diet can have a significant impact on their symptoms and overall quality of life. By focusing on a holistic approach to mental wellness, we can address the connection between nutrition and mental health.

One important aspect of nutrition and mental health is the impact of certain foods on our brain chemistry. Foods rich in omega-3 fatty acids, such as salmon, walnuts, and flaxseeds, have been shown to improve mood and reduce symptoms of depression and anxiety. On the other hand, processed foods high in sugar and unhealthy fats can worsen symptoms of mental illness and lead to mood swings and fatigue. By choosing whole, nutrient-dense foods, individuals can support their mental health and promote a sense of balance and well-being.

In addition to choosing the right foods, it's also important to consider how we eat. Mindful eating practices, such as paying attention to our hunger cues, chewing slowly, and savouring each bite, can help improve digestion and nutrient absorption.

Eating in a calm, relaxed environment can also reduce stress and promote a sense of well-being. By approaching meals with mindfulness and intention, individuals can support their mental health and cultivate a positive relationship with food.

Another key aspect of nutrition and mental health is the gut-brain connection. Research has shown that the health of our gut microbiome plays a significant role in our mental health. Probiotic-rich foods, such as yogurt, kefir, and sauerkraut, can help support a healthy gut and improve mood and cognitive function. By nourishing our gut with probiotics and fibre-rich foods, individuals can support their mental health and reduce symptoms of anxiety and depression.

In conclusion, nutrition is a powerful tool for improving mental health and overall well-being. By choosing whole, nutrient-dense foods, practicing mindful eating habits, and supporting a healthy gut microbiome, individuals can support their mental health and promote a sense of balance and harmony. By taking a holistic approach to mental wellness that includes nutrition, individuals can empower themselves to take control of their mental health and live a fulfilling and vibrant life.

Chapter 4: Healing from Within

Self-Care Practices for Mental Wellness

Self-care practices are essential for maintaining mental wellness, especially for those who are suffering from mental illness. Taking care of yourself is not a luxury, but a necessity in order to promote healing and balance in your life. In this chapter, we will explore some self-care practices that can help you on your journey to holistic mental health.

One important self-care practice for mental wellness is practicing mindfulness. Mindfulness involves being present in the moment and paying attention to your thoughts and feelings without judgment. This practice can help you become more aware of your emotions and reactions, allowing you to respond to difficult situations in a more calm and rational manner. By incorporating mindfulness into your daily routine, you can reduce stress and anxiety, and improve your overall mental well-being.

Another self-care practice that can benefit your mental health is engaging in regular physical activity. Exercise has been shown to have numerous benefits for mental health, including reducing symptoms of depression and anxiety, improving mood, and increasing self-esteem. Whether it's going for a walk, practicing yoga, or hitting the gym, finding an exercise routine that works for you can have a positive impact on your mental well-being.

In addition to mindfulness and physical activity, taking time for relaxation and self-care is crucial for mental wellness. This can include activities such as reading a book, taking a bath, meditating, or spending time in nature. Finding ways to relax and unwind can help you reduce stress, improve sleep, and maintain a sense of balance in your life. Making self-care a priority can help you recharge and rejuvenate both mentally and physically.

Lastly, connecting with others and building a support system is another important self-care practice for mental wellness. Whether it's reaching out to friends and family, joining a support group, or seeking professional help, having a strong support network can provide you with the emotional support and encouragement you need to navigate the challenges of mental illness. By surrounding yourself with positive and understanding individuals, you can feel less isolated and more supported on your journey to holistic mental health.

Building a Support System

One of the most important aspects of maintaining holistic mental wellness is building a strong support system. For people suffering from mental illness, having a network of supportive friends, family members, and professionals can make a world of difference in their journey towards healing. A support system can provide emotional support, practical assistance, and guidance in navigating the challenges of mental illness.

When building a support system, it is important to surround yourself with people who understand and respect your struggles. This may mean seeking out friends or family members who are empathetic and nonjudgmental, as well as mental health professionals who are knowledgeable about holistic approaches to mental wellness. It is also important to communicate your needs and boundaries with your support system, so that they can provide the best possible support for you.

In addition to friends, family, and professionals, it can also be helpful to connect with others who are experiencing similar challenges. Support groups and online communities can provide a sense of belonging and understanding that can be incredibly healing for people suffering from mental illness. These groups can also offer practical advice, coping strategies, and resources for managing symptoms and improving overall mental wellness.

Building a support system is an ongoing process that requires effort and intention. It is important to regularly check in with your support network, express gratitude for their support, and seek out new connections when needed. By surrounding yourself with caring and understanding individuals, you can create a strong foundation for holistic mental wellness and healing.

Overall, building a support system is essential for people suffering from mental illness who are seeking holistic approaches to mental wellness. By cultivating a network of supportive friends, family members, professionals, and peers, individuals can find the strength, guidance, and resources they need to navigate the challenges of mental illness and work towards healing and balance in their lives.

Practicing Gratitude and Mindfulness

Practicing gratitude and mindfulness are two powerful tools that can greatly benefit individuals suffering from mental illness. By incorporating these practices into your daily routine, you can begin to shift your focus away from negative thoughts and emotions, and towards a more positive and balanced mindset.

Gratitude involves acknowledging and appreciating the good things in your life, no matter how small they may seem. By taking the time to reflect on the positive aspects of your day, you can train your brain to become more attuned to the good, rather than the bad. This can help to counteract the negative thought patterns that often accompany mental illness and promote a more optimistic outlook on life.

Mindfulness, on the other hand, is the practice of being fully present in the moment, without judgment or distraction. By cultivating mindfulness in your daily life, you can learn to observe your thoughts and emotions without getting caught up in them. This can help you to develop a greater sense of self-awareness, and to better understand the underlying causes of your mental health struggles.

When combined, gratitude and mindfulness can have a powerful synergistic effect on your mental well-being. By practicing gratitude, you can cultivate a sense of appreciation for the present moment, while mindfulness can help you to stay grounded and centred, even in the face of adversity. Together, these practices can help you to build resilience and cope more effectively with the challenges of mental illness.

Incorporating gratitude and mindfulness into your daily routine may take time and practice, but the benefits are well worth the effort. By making a conscious effort to focus on the positive aspects of your life, and to stay present and aware in each moment, you can begin to cultivate a more balanced and holistic approach to mental wellness. With time and dedication, these practices can help you to find greater peace, happiness, and stability in your life.

Chapter 5: Finding Balance in Daily Life

Time Management and Prioritizing Self-Care

Time management and prioritizing self-care are essential components of holistic mental health. People suffering from mental illness often struggle to find the time and energy to take care of themselves, but it is crucial to make self-care a priority in order to maintain balance and well-being. By effectively managing your time and prioritizing self-care activities, you can improve your mental health and overall quality of life.

One key aspect of time management is setting boundaries and learning to say no when necessary. It can be easy to overcommit yourself and take on too many responsibilities, leading to feelings of overwhelm and burnout. By learning to prioritize your own needs and saying no to things that do not serve your well-being, you can create more time and space for self-care activities that nourish your mind, body, and soul.

Another important aspect of time management is creating a schedule that includes regular self-care practices. This may include activities such as meditation, exercise, journaling, or spending time in nature. By scheduling these activities into your daily or weekly routine, you can ensure that you are making time for yourself and prioritizing your mental health.

Prioritizing self-care also means recognizing when you need to take a break and rest. People suffering from mental illness often experience high levels of stress and anxiety, which can take a toll on their mental and physical health. By listening to your body and mind and taking breaks when needed, you can prevent burnout and maintain a sense of balance in your life.

In conclusion, time management and prioritizing self-care are essential components of holistic mental health. By setting boundaries, creating a schedule that includes self-care activities, and recognizing when you need to take a break, you can improve your mental well-being and overall quality of life. Remember to make yourself a priority and take the time to nourish your mind, body, and soul.

Setting Boundaries and Saying No

Setting boundaries and learning to say no are crucial skills for anyone, especially for those suffering from mental illness. Many people with mental health challenges struggle with people-pleasing tendencies, feeling like they have to say yes to every request or demand placed upon them. This can lead to feeling overwhelmed, resentful, and ultimately worsening mental health symptoms. By setting boundaries and practicing saying no, individuals can regain a sense of control over their lives and prioritize their own well-being.

One key aspect of setting boundaries is recognizing your own limits and needs. It's important to understand what you can realistically handle and what is too much for you to take on. This may involve tuning into your physical and emotional cues, such as feeling drained, anxious, or irritable when you are stretched too thin. By being in tune with your own needs, you can better communicate and enforce your boundaries with others.

Saying no can be challenging, especially for those who are used to saying yes to everything. However, it is a skill that can be developed with practice. It's important to remember that saying no is not a rejection of the other person, but a prioritization of your own needs and well-being. By setting boundaries and saying no, when necessary, you are showing self-respect and self-care.

Setting boundaries can also help to improve relationships with others. When you are clear about your limits and needs, others will have a better understanding of how to interact with you. This can lead to healthier, more respectful relationships where both parties feel heard and respected. By communicating your boundaries effectively, you can create a more harmonious and balanced environment for yourself and those around you.

In conclusion, setting boundaries and saying no are essential practices for anyone looking to improve their mental wellness. By recognizing your limits, prioritizing your own needs, and communicating effectively with others, you can create a healthier and more balanced life. Remember that it is okay to say no and prioritize yourself, as taking care of your own well-being is crucial for managing mental health challenges. Practice setting boundaries and saying no with kindness and compassion towards yourself and watch as your mental wellness improves.

Incorporating Holistic Practices into Your Routine

Incorporating holistic practices into your routine can greatly benefit your mental health. Holistic approaches to mental wellness focus on treating the whole person - mind, body, and spirit - rather than just the symptoms of mental illness. By adopting a holistic approach, you can address the underlying causes of your mental health issues and promote overall well-being.

One way to incorporate holistic practices into your routine is to prioritize self-care. This includes taking time for yourself each day to relax, unwind, and recharge. Whether it's through meditation, yoga, journaling, or simply taking a walk-in nature, finding activities that bring you peace and joy can help reduce stress and improve your mental health.

Another important aspect of holistic mental health is nutrition. Eating a diet rich in whole, nutrient-dense foods can have a significant impact on your mood and overall mental well-being. Foods like fruits, vegetables, whole grains, and lean proteins can help stabilize blood sugar levels and provide the necessary nutrients for optimal brain function.

Physical activity is also essential for holistic mental health. Regular exercise has been shown to reduce symptoms of depression and anxiety, improve sleep quality, and boost overall mood. Whether it's going for a run, practicing yoga, or taking a dance class, finding a form of exercise that you enjoy can have a positive impact on your mental health.

Finally, incorporating holistic practices into your routine also means fostering positive relationships and seeking support from others. Surrounding yourself with friends, family, or a support group who understand and validate your experiences can provide a sense of belonging and connection. Additionally, seeking out holistic healthcare providers such as therapists, nutritionists, or acupuncturists who specialize in holistic approaches can help you develop a personalized plan for improving your mental health.

Chapter 6: Overcoming Mental Health Stigma

Educating Yourself and Others

In order to truly find balance and achieve holistic mental health, it is crucial to educate yourself and others about the various approaches to mental wellness. By understanding different methods and techniques, individuals suffering from mental illness can empower themselves to take control of their own mental health journey. Education is key in breaking down the stigma surrounding mental illness and promoting a more supportive and understanding environment for those struggling.

One important aspect of educating yourself about holistic mental health is to explore different treatment options beyond traditional therapy and medication. This may include practices such as mindfulness, meditation, yoga, and acupuncture. By learning about these alternative approaches, individuals can discover new tools to manage their symptoms and improve their overall well-being. It is important to remember that what works for one person may not work for another, so it is essential to explore different options and find what resonates with you personally.

Educating others about mental health is also crucial in creating a more compassionate and understanding community. By sharing your own experiences and knowledge, you can help break down stereotypes and misconceptions surrounding mental illness. This can help create a more supportive environment for those struggling with their mental health and encourage others to seek help when needed. By raising awareness and promoting open conversations about mental health, we can work towards reducing the stigma and shame often associated with mental illness.

In addition to educating yourself and others about holistic approaches to mental wellness, it is important to prioritize self-care and self-compassion. This may include setting boundaries, practicing self-compassion, and engaging in activities that bring you joy and relaxation. By taking care of yourself and prioritizing your own well-being, you can better cope with the challenges of mental illness and maintain a sense of balance in your life.

Overall, educating yourself and others about holistic mental health is an important step towards finding balance and well-being. By exploring different treatment options, sharing your experiences, and prioritizing self-care, you can empower yourself to take control of your mental health journey and create a more supportive and understanding community for those struggling with mental illness. Remember, you are not alone in this journey, and there is hope and healing available to you.

Advocating for Mental Health Awareness

Advocating for mental health awareness is crucial for those suffering from mental illness, as well as for society as a whole. By raising awareness about mental health issues, we can reduce the stigma surrounding these conditions and encourage individuals to seek help without fear of judgment. It is important for those struggling with mental illness to speak out about their experiences and share their stories to help others realize they are not alone in their struggles. By advocating for mental health awareness, we can create a more supportive and understanding community for those in need.

One way to advocate for mental health awareness is to participate in events and campaigns that promote mental wellness. This could include attending mental health conferences, joining support groups, or even organizing your own mental health awareness event in your community. By actively participating in these activities, you can help educate others about the importance of mental health and encourage them to take care of their own mental well-being.

Another way to advocate for mental health awareness is to use your voice and platform to speak out about the issues facing those with mental illness. Whether it's through writing articles, creating social media posts, or giving talks at local events, sharing your experiences and knowledge about mental health can help break down barriers and misconceptions surrounding these conditions. By speaking up, you can help combat the stigma and discrimination that often prevent individuals from seeking the help they need.

Advocating for mental health awareness also involves supporting holistic approaches to mental wellness. This means recognizing that mental health is not just about treating symptoms, but also about addressing the underlying causes of mental illness and promoting overall well-being. By advocating for holistic approaches, such as mindfulness practices, nutrition, exercise, and therapy, you can help individuals achieve balance and harmony in their lives, leading to improved mental health outcomes.

In conclusion, advocating for mental health awareness is essential for those suffering from mental illness and for society as a whole. By raising awareness, participating in events and campaigns, using your voice to speak out, and supporting holistic approaches to mental wellness, you can help create a more compassionate and understanding community for those in need. Together, we can break down the barriers and stigma surrounding mental health and promote a culture of acceptance, support, and healing for all.

Embracing Your Journey to Wellness

In the journey to holistic mental health, it is essential to embrace every step of the process. For those suffering from mental illness, it can sometimes feel overwhelming to think about all the changes that need to be made in order to achieve wellness. However, by taking it one day at a time and focusing on small victories, you can begin to see progress and feel more empowered in your healing journey.

One important aspect of embracing your journey to wellness is practicing self-compassion. It is easy to be hard on yourself when dealing with mental illness, but it is crucial to remember that healing takes time and that setbacks are a normal part of the process. By being kind to yourself and practicing self-care, you can build resilience and strength to face the challenges that come your way.

Another key component of embracing your journey to wellness is finding a support system. Whether it be friends, family, or a therapist, having people to lean on during difficult times can make a world of difference in your mental health journey.

Surround yourself with individuals who uplift and encourage you, and don't be afraid to ask for help when you need it.

In addition to finding support, incorporating holistic approaches to mental wellness can greatly benefit your overall well-being. This can include practices such as meditation, yoga, nutrition, and mindfulness. By taking a holistic approach to your mental health, you can address the root causes of your symptoms and work towards healing from the inside out.

Finally, remember that your journey to wellness is unique to you. What works for one person may not work for another, so it is important to listen to your body and mind and find what resonates with you. By embracing your journey and staying open to new possibilities, you can discover a path to healing that is fulfilling and sustainable in the long term.

Chapter 7: Maintaining Holistic Mental Health

Monitoring Your Progress and Adjusting Your Plan

Monitoring your progress and adjusting your plan are crucial components of achieving holistic mental wellness. As individuals suffering from mental illness, it is important to keep track of how you are feeling and how your current treatment plan is working for you. By regularly monitoring your progress, you can identify any patterns or triggers that may be affecting your mental health. This self-awareness is key to making informed decisions about your treatment and overall well-being.

One way to monitor your progress is to keep a journal or diary where you can record your thoughts, feelings, and experiences daily. This can help you identify any changes in your mood or behaviour over time. You can also use this journal to track any symptoms you may be experiencing, as well as any factors that may be contributing to your mental health issues. By keeping a record of your mental health journey, you can better understand what works for you and what doesn't.

In addition to keeping a journal, it is important to regularly check in with your mental health professionals to discuss your progress and any changes you may need to make to your treatment plan. Your therapist, psychiatrist, or holistic practitioner can provide valuable insight and guidance on how to adjust your plan to better suit your needs. They can also help you set realistic goals and milestones to work towards, so you can track your progress and celebrate your achievements along the way.

As you continue to monitor your progress and adjust your treatment plan, it is important to practice self-care and prioritize your mental health. This may include incorporating holistic practices such as mindfulness meditation, yoga, nutrition, and exercise into your daily routine. These practices can help promote overall well-being and support your mental health journey. Remember to be patient with yourself and give yourself grace as you work towards finding balance and healing.

In conclusion, monitoring your progress and adjusting your plan are essential steps in achieving holistic mental wellness. By staying self-aware, seeking support from mental health professionals, and practicing self-care, you can make informed decisions about your treatment and overall well-being. Remember that healing is a journey, and it is okay to make changes to your plan as needed. Stay committed to your mental health journey and prioritize your well-being every step of the way.

Continuing Education and Growth

One of the key aspects of finding balance and maintaining holistic mental health is the continual pursuit of education and personal growth. For individuals suffering from mental illness, ongoing education can provide valuable insights into the root causes of their struggles and offer new tools and techniques for managing symptoms. By staying informed about the latest research and developments in the field of mental health, individuals can empower themselves to take control of their own well-being and make informed decisions about their treatment options.

Continuing education can also help individuals suffering from mental illness to develop a greater sense of self-awareness and self-compassion. Through learning about the underlying factors that contribute to their mental health challenges, individuals can gain a deeper understanding of themselves and the ways in which their past experiences and beliefs may be influencing their current state of mind. This increased self-awareness can help individuals to recognize and challenge negative thought patterns and behaviours, leading to greater emotional resilience and a more positive outlook on life.

In addition to formal education, personal growth activities such as journaling, mindfulness meditation, and creative expression can also play a vital role in promoting holistic mental wellness. These activities can help individuals to cultivate a sense of inner peace and connectedness, as well as develop important skills such as emotional regulation, stress management, and problem-solving. By making time for personal growth activities on a regular basis, individuals can nurture their mental health and build a strong foundation for long-term well-being.

It is important for individuals suffering from mental illness to remember that growth and healing are ongoing processes that require patience, perseverance, and self-compassion. While setbacks and challenges may arise along the way, it is important to view these obstacles as opportunities for learning and growth rather than reasons to give up. By approaching their journey towards holistic mental health with an open mind and a willingness to learn and grow, individuals can create lasting positive change in their lives and experience greater peace and fulfilment.

In conclusion, continuing education and personal growth are essential components of finding balance and achieving holistic mental wellness. By staying informed about the latest research and developments in the field of mental health, cultivating self-awareness and self-compassion, and engaging in personal growth activities, individuals suffering from mental illness can empower themselves to take control of their well-being and create a more fulfilling and meaningful life. Remember, the journey towards holistic mental health is a marathon, not a sprint – so be patient with yourself, stay committed to your growth, and never give up on the possibility of a brighter tomorrow.

Celebrating Your Successes and Practicing Self-Compassion

In the journey to holistic mental wellness, it's essential to celebrate your successes, no matter how big or small they may seem. Oftentimes, those suffering from mental illness can be too hard on themselves and fail to recognize the progress they have made. Taking the time to acknowledge and celebrate your achievements can help boost your self-esteem and confidence, leading to improved mental well-being. Whether it's getting out of bed in the morning or completing a task that seemed daunting, every accomplishment deserves to be recognized and celebrated.

Practicing self-compassion is another key aspect of finding balance in your mental health journey. It's important to treat yourself with kindness and understanding, especially when facing challenges or setbacks. Instead of being self-critical or judgmental, try to show yourself the same compassion you would offer to a friend in need. This can help you cultivate a more positive self-image and foster a sense of inner peace and acceptance. By practicing self-compassion, you can learn to be more forgiving of yourself and let go of negative self-talk that may be holding you back.

One way to celebrate your successes and practice self-compassion is by keeping a gratitude journal. Writing down three things you are grateful for each day can help shift your focus from what's going wrong to what's going right in your life. This simple practice can help cultivate a more positive mindset and improve your overall well-being. Additionally, taking time to reflect on your accomplishments and showing yourself kindness can help you build resilience and cope with the challenges that come your way.

Another way to celebrate your successes and practice self-compassion is by engaging in self-care activities that bring you joy and relaxation. Whether it's taking a long bath, going for a walk-in nature, or indulging in your favourite hobby, prioritizing self-care can help you recharge and rejuvenate both mentally and physically. Remember that self-care is not selfish but essential for maintaining your well-being. By taking care of yourself, you are better equipped to handle the ups and downs of life and navigate the challenges of mental illness with grace and resilience.

In conclusion, celebrating your successes and practicing self-compassion are essential components of finding balance in your mental health journey. By acknowledging your achievements, showing yourself kindness, and engaging in self-care activities, you can cultivate a more positive mindset and improve your overall well-being. Remember to be gentle with yourself, celebrate your progress, and prioritize self-care as you work towards holistic mental wellness. You are worthy of love, compassion, and happiness – so be sure to treat yourself with the care and kindness you deserve.

Chapter 8: Resources for Holistic Mental Health

Finding Holistic Mental Health Practitioners

When seeking treatment for mental illness, it is essential to consider holistic approaches that address the mind, body, and spirit. Holistic mental health practitioners take into account the interconnectedness of these aspects of wellness and offer a comprehensive approach to healing. In this subchapter, we will explore how to find holistic mental health practitioners who can support you on your journey to mental wellness.

One of the first steps in finding a holistic mental health practitioner is to research different modalities and approaches to mental wellness. Holistic practitioners may specialize in a variety of techniques such as acupuncture, yoga, meditation, nutrition, or energy healing. It is important to find a practitioner whose approach resonates with you and aligns with your personal beliefs and values.

Another important factor to consider when searching for a holistic mental health practitioner is their credentials and experience. Look for practitioners who have specialized training in holistic approaches to mental health and who have a proven track record of helping clients achieve positive outcomes. It may also be helpful to read reviews and testimonials from other clients to get a sense of their effectiveness and professionalism.

When reaching out to potential holistic mental health practitioners, be sure to ask about their treatment philosophy and approach. A good practitioner will take the time to listen to your concerns, assess your needs, and work collaboratively with you to develop a personalized treatment plan. Trust your instincts and choose a practitioner who makes you feel comfortable, supported, and empowered on your healing journey.

In conclusion, finding a holistic mental health practitioner who can support you on your path to mental wellness is an important step in your healing journey. By researching different modalities, considering credentials and experience, and exploring treatment philosophies, you can find a practitioner who aligns with your goals and values. Remember that healing is a personal and unique journey, and finding the right practitioner can make all the difference in your mental health and well-being.

Recommended Reading and Websites

For those seeking to explore holistic approaches to mental wellness, there are a plethora of resources available to help guide you on your journey towards finding balance and healing. Here are some recommended reading materials and websites that provide valuable information and support for people suffering from mental illness.

One highly recommended book **is "The Mindful Way Through Depression" by Mark Williams, John Teasdale,**

Zindel Segal, and Jon Kabat-Zinn. This groundbreaking book offers a mindfulness-based approach to dealing with depression and has helped countless individuals find relief from their symptoms. The authors provide practical exercises and techniques that can be incorporated into daily life to promote emotional well-being and resilience.

Another excellent resource is the **website Psychology Today**, which offers a wealth of articles and information on various holistic approaches to mental health. From mindfulness practices to nutrition tips, Psychology Today covers a wide range of topics that can help individuals manage their mental health in a holistic and integrated way.

For those interested in exploring the connection between mental health and spirituality, the book **"The Untethered Soul" by Michael A. Singer** is a great read. This transformative book explores the power of mindfulness and meditation in helping individuals navigate the challenges of life and find inner peace and balance.

If you are looking for a comprehensive guide to holistic mental health, the **website Holistic Mental Health** offers a wealth of resources, including articles, videos, and online courses. This site covers a range of topics, from alternative therapies to lifestyle changes that can support mental well-being and help individuals achieve a sense of balance and wholeness.

In conclusion, finding balance and healing from mental illness requires a holistic approach that addresses the mind, body, and spirit. By exploring the recommended reading materials and websites mentioned above, individuals can gain valuable insights and tools to help them on their journey towards wellness. Remember, you are not alone in your struggles, and there are resources available to support you every step of the way.

Support Groups and Community Resources

Support groups and community resources play a crucial role in the journey towards holistic mental wellness. For people suffering from mental illness, finding a supportive community can provide much-needed validation, understanding, and encouragement. By connecting with others who are facing similar challenges, individuals can gain a sense of belonging and reduce feelings of isolation. Support groups also offer a safe space to share experiences, exchange coping strategies, and receive valuable feedback from peers who can relate to their struggles.

One of the key benefits of support groups is the opportunity to learn from others who have successfully navigated the complexities of mental illness. Hearing stories of resilience and recovery can inspire hope and motivation, helping individuals see that it is possible to overcome their challenges and live a fulfilling life. In addition, support groups often provide access to valuable resources and information about holistic approaches to mental wellness, including alternative therapies, self-care practices, and lifestyle modifications that can complement traditional treatment methods.

Community resources are another important aspect of holistic mental health care, offering a wide range of services and programs to support individuals on their healing journey. These resources may include mental health clinics, counselling centres, wellness workshops, and educational seminars focused on promoting mental well-being. By taking advantage of these resources, individuals can access professional guidance, learn new skills, and gain valuable insights into managing their mental health in a holistic and sustainable way.

In addition to support groups and community resources, individuals suffering from mental illness can also benefit from engaging in activities that promote connection, creativity, and self-expression. Art therapy, yoga, meditation, nature walks, and volunteer work are just a few examples of holistic practices that can nourish the mind, body, and spirit. By exploring different avenues for self-care and personal growth, individuals can discover new sources of joy, meaning, and purpose in their lives, leading to a greater sense of balance and well-being.

In conclusion, support groups and community resources are invaluable tools for individuals seeking holistic approaches to mental wellness. By connecting with others who understand their struggles, accessing professional guidance and information, and engaging in activities that promote self-care and personal growth, individuals can cultivate a sense of empowerment, resilience, and hope in the face of mental illness. By embracing a holistic approach to mental health care, individuals can create a foundation for long-term well-being and fulfilment, taking control of their own healing journey and finding balance in mind, body, and spirit.

Community Resources:

Contact your own country's / community's Mental Health Services if you need help. Please don't be afraid to reach out!

Mental Health Foundation of New Zealand:

Need to talk? any time for support from a trained counsellor.

LIFELINE - 0800 543 354 (0800 LIFELINE) or free text 4357 (HELP).

YOUTHLINE - 0800 376 633, free text 234 or email talk@youthline.co.nz or online chat.

SAMARITANS - 0800 726 666

SUICIDE CRISIS HELPLINE - 0508 828 865 (0508 TAUTOKO).

Conclusion: Embracing Your Journey to Holistic Mental Health

In conclusion, embracing your journey to holistic mental health is a powerful and transformative process that can lead to lasting healing and well-being. By incorporating holistic approaches to mental wellness into your daily routine, you can cultivate a sense of balance and harmony in all aspects of your life. From practicing mindfulness and meditation to nourishing your body with whole foods and engaging in regular physical activity, there are countless ways to support your mental health naturally.

One of the key components of holistic mental health is recognizing the interconnectedness of the mind, body, and spirit. When we focus on healing all aspects of ourselves, we can experience profound shifts in our mental health and overall well-being. By taking a holistic approach to mental wellness, we can address the root causes of our mental health struggles and create lasting change from the inside out.

It's important to remember that embracing your journey to holistic mental health is not a quick fix or a one-size-fits-all solution. It requires dedication, patience, and a willingness to explore new ways of thinking and being. By committing to your own healing journey and seeking support from holistic practitioners, therapists, and other like-minded individuals, you can create a powerful foundation for lasting mental wellness.

As you continue your journey to holistic mental health, remember to be gentle with yourself and practice self-compassion. Healing is a process, and it's okay to have setbacks and challenges along the way. By staying committed to your own well-being and taking small steps each day towards greater balance and harmony, you can create a life filled with joy, purpose, and inner peace.

In closing, I encourage you to embrace your journey to holistic mental health with an open heart and an open mind. By integrating holistic approaches to mental wellness into your daily life, you can cultivate a sense of wholeness and well-being that will empower you to thrive in all areas of your life. Remember, you are worthy of healing and happiness, and your journey to holistic mental health is a powerful step towards creating the life you truly deserve.

The Four Dimensions of Hauora (Holistic Wellbeing)

- **Taha tinana** - physical wellbeing: The physical body, its growth, development, and ability to move, and ways of caring for it.

- **Taha hinengaro** - mental and emotional wellbeing: Coherent thinking processes, acknowledging and expressing thoughts and feelings and responding constructively.

- **Taha whānau** - social wellbeing: **whānau** (family) relationships, friendships, and other interpersonal relationships; feelings of belonging, compassion and caring; and social support.

- **Taha wairua** - spiritual wellbeing: The values and beliefs that determine the way people live, the search for meaning and purpose in life, and personal identity and self-awareness.

Māori Meeting House:

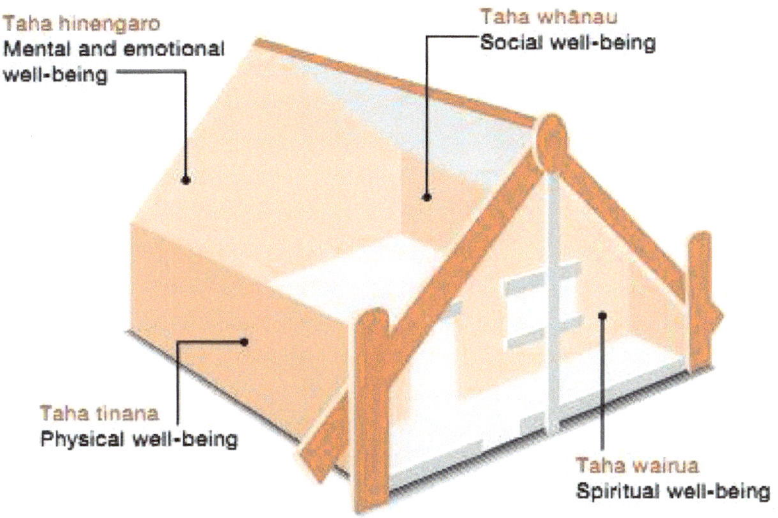

Image used from New Zealand Ministry of Education